THE
PYRGIC
PUZZLER

CLASSIC CONUNDRUMS

CHRISTOPHER MASLANKA

Illustrations by Michael Harrington
Foreword by Iris Murdoch

DOVER PUBLICATIONS, INC.
Mineola, New York

Bibliographical Note

The Pyrgic Puzzler, first published by Dover Publications, Inc., in 2011, is an unabridged republication of the work originally published by The Kingswood Press, William Heinemann Ltd., London, in 1987. A new Introduction has been written by the author for the Dover edition.

Library of Congress Cataloging-in-Publication Data

Maslanka, Christopher.
    The pyrgic puzzler : classic conundrums / Christopher Maslanka ; illustrations by Michael Harrington ; foreword by Iris Murdoch.
        p. cm.
        ISBN-13: 978-0-486-48453-2
        ISBN-10: 0-486-48453-X
        1. Puzzles. I. Title.

GV1493 .M295 2011
793.73—dc23

2011036109

Manufactured in the United States by Courier Corporation
48453X01
www.doverpublications.com

For John Simopoulos

I extend my thanks to Matthew Jolly, James Briscoe, Gerald Fitzalan Howard, Andy Sphyris, and all my other pupils for their lively sense of paradox. To the readers of *The Oxford Mail* and *The New Scientist* whose letters to me testified to the enjoyment and amusement to be had from puzzle-solving. To Demetrios Nianias for his pyrgic encouragement and finally to Ione Noble for all her help and understanding throughout the production of the book.

CONTENTS

I confess I am not a great solver of puzzles. I look with admiration upon the ingenuity of the author of these, and extend my sympathetic applause to the innumerable people who will seize upon them with glee and solve them with satisfaction. In these mental acrobatics, old and young compete on equal terms, except perhaps that the very young may have an advantage. A stylish and elegant book for the computer age; but not just that. There is a degree of surrealist teasing involved, so enthusiasts must be ready to change gear and not try to be too clever. The vivid explanatory pictures are of course a necessary part of the enterprise – indeed a study of them is essential – and the engaging and charmingly named characters soon become one's personal friends. In fact one can soon drift away dreamily into this lucidly imagined and perilous world. Perhaps Mr Maslanka has created a literary form. The little tales, so witty, so disconcerting, so every-day, may remind one of Kafka, and the book may be 'read as literature' just as in the case of Wittgenstein's *Tractatus* or the Bible. May we not hope for more from the pen of clever Mr Maslanka and his talented illustrator? Possibly a novel? I must consult Mr Maslanka's wise friend, Mr Telephonopoulos.

Iris Murdoch

PREFACE

I have sometimes been accused of writing rather difficult
puzzles, and, I realise that there may be occasions when some
people might feel they need a little help. For them, I have
provided a selection of hints for the more difficult puzzles
(marked with **H**), which appears before the answer section.
They should put the aspiring puzzle-solver on the right path.
Nor have I forgotten those mathematical whizz-kids: for them,
there is an appendix which explains, in greater depth the
answers to the puzzles (see those marked with **A**).

Christopher Maslanka
Oxford
February 1987

INTRODUCTION TO THE DOVER EDITION

Some thirty years after the *Pyrgic Puzzler* was written, it is curious to think that a book that has so completely transformed my life was originally not written for publication at all, but as a diverting travelling companion for a friend.

An academic acquaintance of mine from Oxford was due to fly to Greece to spend two weeks in a tower of the kind that the inhabitants of the islands of Chios and Lesvos call a *Pyrgos*. Now, my friend is not a good traveller: no sooner has he arrived somewhere than he wishes himself back home.

As the date of departure approached, he became more and more anxious. I wrote a set of puzzles that would both absorb and distract him in his tower. As these puzzles were set in the familiar world of Oxford, he only needed to read one of them to be at once transported home, if only in his imagination. Thus were the *Pyrgic Puzzles* born.

The puzzles proved a great success, and on my friend's return, they found a home on his coffee table in his rooms in Oxford, where he taught philosophy. Diligent pupils were occasionally rewarded with one of the puzzles.

And so matters might have rested, had Iris Murdoch not dropped by to visit just as my friend was called away to the telephone. When he returned, he found the great novelist comfortably ensconced on his sofa deeply absorbed in the puzzles. She told my friend that they should be published.

After the book came out, the question of what I was to do for a career settled itself. There were newspaper columns, consultations, radio programmes, and huge numbers of letters to answer from members of the public correcting, informing, enquiring, or just quibbling: all about puzzles.

If my friend had not been called away to the phone at that precise moment, Iris Murdoch might not have picked up the puzzles. Then I would not have embarked on a life that culminated with an Oxford College appointing me its College Enigmatist (a unique post not unlike that of a medieval court jester, but without the attendant political risk). Henceforth my work would be play; and my play would be work.

It is an honour for *The Pyrgic Puzzler* to find a new home in the country that gave birth, among others, to the great puzzlist Sam Loyd, the late-lamented Martin Gardner, and Ray Smullyan. May these puzzles now amuse and transport American readers, just as they once did my academic friend in his lonely tower in Lesvos!

Chris Maslanka
College Enigmatist of St Catherine's College, Oxford

THE PYRGIC PUZZLER

CLASSIC CONUNDRUMS

A man, feeling tired of the life he had been living, was surprised to receive a letter from a friend inviting him to cast off all his cares and come and stay in a far-off land in a tall tower (or pyrgos) overlooking the world below.

'Viewed from on high, your preoccupations will shrink . . .', the letter read.

He sat down in a comfortable armchair and pondered on how little he knew of the land to which his friend proposed a visit. What of all the friends and acquaintances he would be leaving behind? Would it be wise to undertake a journey into a strange land of whose customs and inhabitants he was so ignorant? Would it be wise to engage in such an adventure with all its attendant mysteries and perils both real and imaginary? And it was no use pretending that the imaginary ones were any less real. So he pondered. . . .

1   Colonel Plantpott-Smythe was daydreaming in his favourite armchair by the potted palm at The Old India Club when his reveries of distant lands were interrupted by a voice saying, 'Although you have no children, my dear Cruddington, that girl's uncle is the brother of your brother's sister.'

About whom was the unseen speaker speaking?

2   A says to B, 'Will you marry me?'

     B replies to him, 'Yes, but I won't be your wife.'

     Explain this.

3   X says to Y, 'You are my wife.'

     Y replies to X, 'You are not my husband.'

     Explain this.

4   Professor Pembish, astronomer and eccentric, is extremely
    fond of sunbathing. His house has been built to his own
    careful specifications and has windows in every wall to
    catch the sun. All its windows face south.

    How is this possible?

5   Pembish has another house in which all the windows face
    east.

    How is this possible?

6   On Zircon the currency is such that 11 dinglies make a dong, the dingly being the smallest unit of money. A party of clones enters a coffee shop and spend altogether 10 dongs and 8 dinglies.

One clone says to the others, 'I can remember a time when coffee was only a dingly, but now everything is so expensive.'

Now, as the distinctive thing about clones is that they are all identical and all do exactly the same, the others were all equally surprised to hear one of their number saying something that the rest of them were not.

'Why are you telling me that?' they all piped up simultaneously.

How many clones were there in the party and how much did they each spend? **H**

7   To amuse his sister's baby boy Professor Puttylump drops a soft ball of jumblium on the floor. This brightly coloured metal always bounces up to a height exactly half the height from which it falls.

The boy gurgles with delight and watches the bright metallic ball bouncing. He then looks puzzled and asks his uncle, 'Da, if you drop it from a height of one metre, how far will it travel *in toto* before coming to rest?'

Now Uncle Putty had no idea where *Toto* was, but he did know the answer to the question.

What was it?

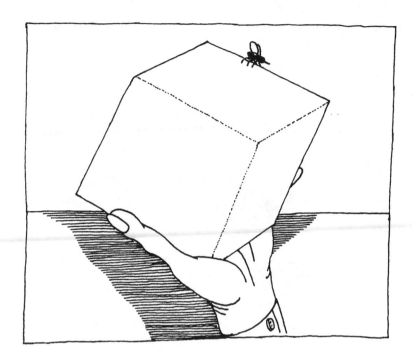

8   Professor Mozzarella has a low opinion of his nephew's mathematical abilities. He asked the boy the following question: 'A small fly starts walking from one corner of a sugar cube, and, confining herself to its edges, which are all exactly one centimetre long, walks as far as she possibly can without retracing any part of her path. How far does she walk?'

The nephew answered with a confident grin: '12 centimetres.'

What *should* he have answered?

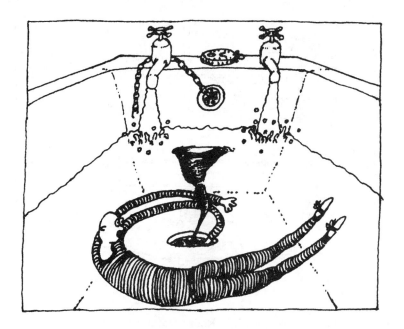

9   Professor Pembish knows that his bath fills in three minutes if the cold tap only is turned on full, and in four minutes if the hot tap only is turned on full. With the plug out, the bath empties in two minutes. One day he finds to his horror that Mrs Oldham has mislaid the plug, but he is intelligent enough to realise that he can still manage to fill the bath with both taps on full.

How long will it take to fill?

10   One day Cryogenes T. Rosencrumpett arrived at the laboratory to find that his technician had left the refrigerator door open.

When he pointed this out the man replied coolly, 'It was such a hot day and I wanted to lower the temperature of the room a bit.'

Why did Cryogenes become heated?   **H**

11   Cryogenes was in the warm laboratory and, being thirsty, took two ice-cubes and put them into a glass. He found there was just enough Spa water left in the refrigerator to fill the glass up to the brim with the ice-cubes floating on the surface.

'Ooh, you'd better drink that before the ice-cubes melt,' said the technician (whose name, by the way, is Rufus T. Apfelsaft). 'Otherwise it will overflow.'

Was he right?　**H**

12   One morning Cryogenes woke and found he had a cold.
      He telephoned the laboratory to tell his technician to
      maintain at a constant temperature the specimen of
      jumblium currently under examination. To make sure the
      man had understood, Cryogenes repeated the vital figure.

      'Yes, yes,' replied the technician, 'but was that Fahrenheit
      or Centigrade?'

      'It makes absolutely no difference,' snapped Cryogenes,
      becoming exasperated.

      What was the temperature?   **H**

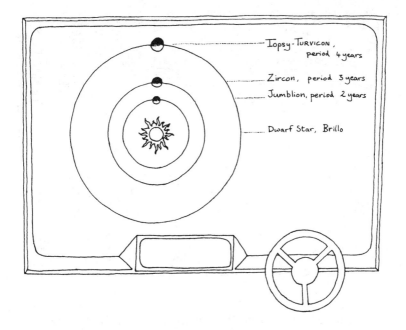

Topsy-Turvicon, period 4 years

Zircon, period 3 years

Jumblion, period 2 years

Dwarf Star, Brillo

13 The planets Zircon, Topsy-Turvicon and Jumblion move
in circular orbits centred on the dwarf star Brillo, and with
orbital periods of three years, four years and two years
respectively. In the year 2001, the four bodies all lie along
a straight line.

In what year will these four celestial bodies next all lie in a
straight line? **H**

14   Russell asked Moore how many apples he had in his basket. Moore replied that if he had 1½ apples more he would have 1½ times as many.

How many had he?

15　Puttylump's wife likes horse-racing, a sport for which
Uncle Putty finds himself unable to develop much
enthusiasm. On the occasions when his wife goes off to
the races he generally spends his time wandering around
Little Biddings musing to himself. On one such occasion
he met and struck up a conversation with a farmer leaning
on his hen-coop.

'Now these 'ere 'ens are very productive,' said the
farmer, beaming with pride and affection. 'Most 'ens only
lays one egg a day. But these. . . . Why, do you know,'
(at this point he leant towards Puttylump as if letting him
into a secret), 'if I raise the number of 'ens I 'ave, to the
power of the number of eggs they each produces in a day,
I get the same number I'd get if I raised the number of
eggs they produces in a day to the power of the number of
'ens I 'ave? There's a coincidence for you! From the point
of view of feedin' 'em, of course, it would be cheaper if
the number of 'ens and the number of eggs they each lay
were swapped round, but you can't 'ave everything.'

The professor raised an eyebrow and reached for his
calculator.

How many hens did the farmer have, and how many eggs
did they each lay in a day?　**H**

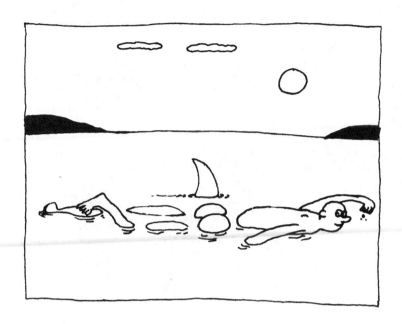

16   A fitness fanatic can swim at twice the speed of the
prevailing tide. He swims out to a buoy and back again,
taking four minutes in all.

How long would it take him in still water? **H**

17   In Zarkov, I am told, the main coin in currency is the
     zolot, which, like the five-zolot piece, is worth its weight
     in gold.

     Which is worth more: a kilogram of zolots or a kilogram of
     five-zolot pieces?

18 Jumblium is a curious metal: it shrinks when heated and expands on cooling, whereas most metals, like iron, do the opposite. Rufus T. Apfelsaft knew this much, so when Cryogenes asked him to heat an iron washer and cool a jumblium washer, he already had a good idea of what would happen to the size of the holes in the washers in the process.

What *does* happen to them?

19   It takes one bale of hay and seven turnips to feed
     adequately three cows in a herd of the identical cows of
     Tradescantius. To feed four such cows, two bales of hay
     would suffice with the same number of turnips as before.

     If there was no hay, how many turnips would be required
     to feed six cows?

20   'What number,' asked Professor Didipotamus, absent-mindedly trying to wind up his snuff-box, 'must be added to the numerator and to the denominator of the fraction ¼ to give the fraction ⅔?'

'Well?' he said finally, replacing his snuff-box in his jacket pocket and tugging out his watch.

Well? **H**

21 'What I find most difficult about your language,' someone
remarked to Szklowski, 'is all the consonants; it's so
difficult to read. Take the word ''skrzypki'', for instance.
What does it mean?'

'Violin, old boy,' replied the Man from All Souls with the
transparent walking-stick. 'But Polish is by no means
unique in this respect. Why, only today in London I saw a
place-name with six consecutive consonants in its
spelling.'

'Really, what was that?'

At this point, a loud sneeze obscured Szklowski's reply.
What was it?

22　'There are few Polish words of two letters,' said
Szklowski as the waiter brought in their coffee, 'and there
is only one English noun of two letters.'

'That must be ''id'',' said the astronomer, Seymour Stars.

'No, I had in mind a *common* English noun,' said
Szklowski with great emphasis. 'So that rules out nouns
such as ai, em, en, mu and zo. . . .'

What was the word Szklowski had in mind?

23   Not to be outdone by a man with a transparent walking-stick, Dr Stars beards him over coffee.

'Tell me, then, a word, which, if printed in block capitals down a page, will read exactly the same when viewed in a mirror.'

Szklowski immediately gave six while stirring his coffee.

What might they have been?

24 'If you look at that bottle standing on the table over there,' remarked Stars, 'you will observe that the word HOCK, printed across the label in block capitals, appears unchanged on reflection in the polished surface of the table.'

'Yes,' piped up an undergraduette as they sat down with their coffee, 'and if you look out of the window you will see a tree whose name, if printed in block capitals across the page, would also read exactly the same when viewed upside down in a mirror.'

Stars looked out of the window and saw a tree. What sort of tree was it? **H**

25 'A propos your question about the six consecutive consonants,' said John Bayleaf, who had been waiting longest for his coffee, 'can you think of a five-letter English word consisting of one consonant followed by four vowels?'

26   Dr Stars seemed to be quite taken with the under-graduette, who was a guest of John Bayleaf. He wanted to ask her age, but not wishing to appear rude, he asked her instead to reverse the digits in her age and add the resulting number to her age. He then asked her to tell him the largest number less than 11 by which the final result was divisible. The undergraduette replied that this number was 10. Stars, knowing that she must be younger than 28, then knew her age at once.

What was it? **H**

27 In response to the girl's enquiring look, Stars went slightly pink and said, 'Although I feel I am in the prime of life, my age in years is not a prime number, and, although I am not at all odd,' (at this point Szklowski coughed loudly), 'my age is an odd number. If you do a similar calculation to the one you just did on your age, but on mine, you end up with a perfect square.'

He looked at Szklowski before continuing. 'I don't mind the calculation producing a perfect square,' he sighed. 'But how I wish my age were once again divisible by four as well!'

How old is Stars, and how much younger did he wish that he might have been? **H**

28 'Problems, eh?' said Mr Telephonopoulos, joining them for coffee and changing the subject to telephones.

'Can you,' he said, addressing Dr Stars, 'using as many addition and multiplication signs as you like, make the number 100 by combining the numbers on a telephone dial and using each digit once and once only?'

Dr Stars blushed. Can you?

29 'Well,' said Telephonopoulos beaming, 'you solved that quickly enough, so you had better try another problem. To obtain the sum of all the digits on a telephone dial, you just add them together. To get the product of all the digits on a telephone dial, you multiply them together. What is the result of taking the sum of all the digits on a telephone dial and multiplying this by their product?'

Dr Stars started to scribble away on the back of an envelope, but the undergraduette beat him to the answer.

What was it?

30 'Well,' said Stars, 'at least I managed to find the *sum* of
the digits on a telephone dial, even if I wasn't able to
proceed much further. It's 45.'

'If you know that, you are already half-way towards
solving this next problem,' said Telephonopoulos. 'Can
you make the number 100 using only addition signs and
each of the digits on a telephone dial once and once only?'

Stars evidently brought his mind to bear on this problem,
for he was able to answer it in just under a minute.

What is the answer? **H**

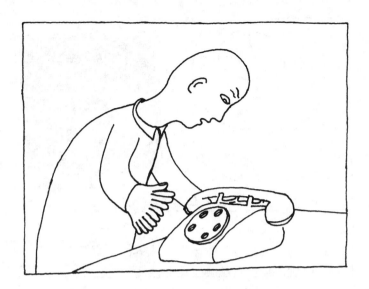

31 'Speaking of the numbers on a telephone dial,' said the undergraduette to Mr Telephonopoulos, 'which of the digits 0 to 9 appears least and which appears most in the numbers from 1 to 100 inclusive?'

Well?

32   'More coffee?' asked Szklowski, offering Stars the coffee and cream.

'Thank you,' blinked Stars. 'Without cream, please. I've taken to having my coffee black and unsweetened.'

'Hm,' said Szklowski. 'Last night there was no cream, only milk, and I was having none of that, so I had mine black and unsweetened. But I'm certainly making up for it now,' he said, adding extra sugar to his already creamy coffee. 'Still, everyone drank something. Of the 13 who took coffee, 12 took milk and 10 took sugar.'

'Oh, and how many took *all three*?' blinked Stars.

'You tell me!' replied Szklowski.   **H**

33 'That reminds me,' said John Bayleaf, 'of a time when I was giving three guests after-dinner coffee and I called out from the kitchen to see how they wanted it. Back came the reply that two wanted it with cream, two with sugar, two with rum and none with all three. For a moment I was at a loss as to how to prepare those three cups. But not for long.'

How *did* he prepare them?

34 At this moment the conversation was interrupted by a
    loud 'Cuckoo'. Dr Chronos had just entered with a large
    cuckoo clock under his arm.

    'Your clock is not exactly right,' said Stars.

    'Well, it's not exactly wrong either,' said Chronos, sitting
    down next to Mr Striker, who was puffing away on a
    cigarette. 'You see this is a very special clock: the hands
    show the right time, but the cuckoo only emerges to sing
    when the hands on the clock-face coincide.'

    If the bird was on time and the time was *roughly* 2 pm,
    what time was it *exactly*?

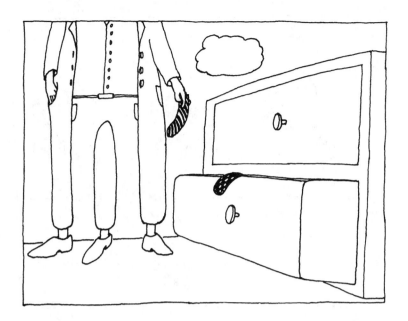

35 John Bayleaf often wears odd socks, and this afternoon
was no exception. He tells me that he keeps all his socks
in a bottom drawer and that when he dresses he removes
a pair at random.

If he has four pairs of socks – one black, one white, one
red and one blue – how many days per week on average
will he be found wearing a conventional pair?

36   Mr Striker has been trying for some time now to give up
      smoking. As part of his displacement activity he plays
      with matches.

      'Here are 12 matches,' he says to Chronos, using the 13th
      to light another cigarette. 'Now arrange them on the table-
      top to make five squares. The matches must not overlap
      and you mustn't break them.' He pauses while Chronos
      moves the matches about on the table.

      'Oh, you managed that,' says Striker. 'Well, in that case,
      how would you go about making six equal squares?'

      Well, how would you?   **H**

37   By the time Chronos had finished the previous problem, Mr Striker had managed to smoke several more cigarettes and this leaves him with only six matches. Unabashed, he challenges Chronos to make four equilateral triangles with them without breaking any of them or allowing them to overlap.

How may it be done? **H**

38 Mr Striker remembers at this point that he had started out with 12 matches, but having smoked another two cigarettes during the course of the last problem, he is now left with only four matches.

Can you help him to use these four remaining matches to write the number 12 without breaking any of them? **H**

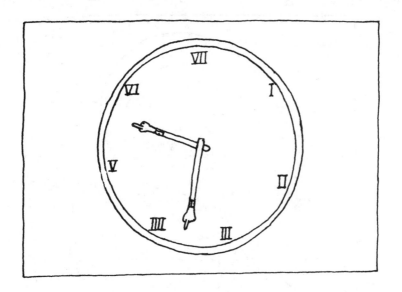

39 'I too am fond of problems,' said Dr Chronos to Mr
Striker, 'but only clock problems, really. For instance, take
a look at this little clock.'

At this point he drew out a rather special clock with the
numbers 1 to 7 inclusive inscribed around its face.

'Each hour on this clock is equal in duration to the hour
on a normal clock. The difference is that it takes only
seven hours for the little hand to make a complete circuit
of the face instead of 12 as on a normal clock. I set the
thing right at midnight every Sunday so that I won't be
late for work on Monday morning. It normally keeps very
good time.'

'But there isn't a number 12 on it,' protested Striker
weakly, 'so how can you set it right at midnight?'

'That's easy enough. On Sunday, when midnight arrives,
I set both the big and the little hand on 7,' said Chronos,
as if to a child. 'Then I know, for instance, that if on a
Thursday afternoon it says 5.30, then it's really . . . well,
you tell me!'   **H**

40   'Well, in that case, what time is it now?' said Striker,
noting that the wall-clock said 2 pm.

'Time to be off,' said Chronos, picking up his cuckoo clock
from the seat beside him and tucking it under his arm.
'It's Thursday, and I have an appointment this afternoon
in town. My seven-hour clock stopped this morning and I
have to take it to the menders. Look, it says 1 pm now.'
With this he swept out, making a timely exit.

When had the clock stopped? **H**

HOW MANY
CIGARS
HAVE YOU
SMOKED TODAY
?

41   Colonel Plantpott-Smythe is about to doze off down at
The Old India Club when he notices Cruddington settling
down in a neighbouring armchair. Knowing that the man
is trying to give up smoking cigars he passes him a note:

Cruddington sighs, scrawls a reply on the back of the card
and returns it. When old Plantpott reads the message (see
below) he is quite taken aback until he realises his mistake.

What was his mistake?

240

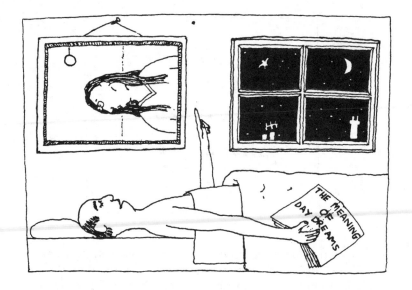

42   Once Cruddington awoke from a peculiar dream in which
      he found himself saying to a girl, 'My dear, your mother
      was my mother's only daughter.'

      What relation was the girl to Cruddington?

43 A says to B, on the occasion of their common birthday,
    'When I reach your age you will be three times as old as I
    was when you were my age now. But please don't feel too
    bad about it; we really are the youngest we could be
    under the circumstances.'

    How old are A and B? **H**

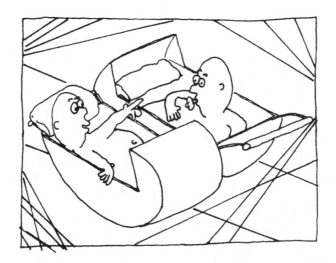

44 A says to B, 'If I were your age I would be three times as
    old as I am.'

    B replies, 'Yes, and if I were as old as you are I'd have to
    wait 15 years to be half as old as I am now.'

    How old are they? **H**

45 When Pembish moved into Pembish Hall, he found that the grounds were littered with cannonballs.

'You should get shot of those,' said Punnish, the old retainer. 'I can tell you where to put them!'

Pembish gritted his teeth, but Punnish continued, 'If you were on the ball you'd cut them in half and use them to edge the driveway.'

'Well,' replied Pembish, 'I've already bought exactly the right amount of bright blue protective paint to paint them as they stand' (at this point Punnish almost interrupted him) '– 10 tins. If you can tell me how many extra tins I'd need to paint them if I bisected them all as you suggest, I might consider following your advice instead of just firing you. . . .'

While Punnish was scratching his head, Pembish ducked into the conservatory.

How many extra tins *would* he have needed? **H**

46   Pembish decided to gather up all the cannonballs and to
      stack them in one large heap. Each layer of cannonballs
      formed a square and each layer had one cannonball less
      along its edge than the layer immediately below it. When
      he had finished there were exactly 30 complete layers, the
      uppermost containing just one cannonball.

      While Pembish was adjusting the last one on the top of his
      pyramidal masterpiece, Punnish tore around the corner of
      the conservatory on a dilapidated penny farthing and
      cannoned into him, sending him and several layers of his
      handiwork rolling on the ground.

      'It would have been better,' Punnish began, 'if you
      pardon my saying so,' (Pembish wasn't sure he would) 'if
      you had made two exactly equal piles of the same shape
      as the one you already have (or had, should I say) and
      then you could have put one heap on either side of the
      door!'

      'I presume you mean "one on *each* side of the door",'
      snapped Pembish, who felt that the long fuse of his
      patience had almost burnt up. 'Besides,' he added with a
      flash of inspiration, 'I'm not at all sure that it would be
      possible.' Punnish scratched his head.

      Leaving aside the aesthetic question, would it be possible,
      in principle, to follow Punnish's advice?

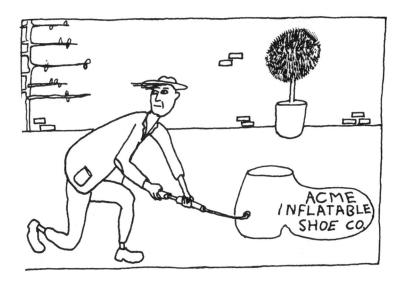

47   Punnish's penny farthing (of which its owner says, 'I
bought it because that's exactly how much it cost me') has
two wheels with solid leather tyres.

'None of that modern inflatable nonsense for me, sir,' he
says to Pembish one fine day. 'If you don't let 'em down,
they'll let you down. If leather's good enough for shoes,
it's good enough for bicycle tyres. Besides we'd look silly
with inflatable soles. . . .'

Pembish cannot help noticing, as the retainer is burbling
on in the background about 'the holes left in the sky by
aeroplanes', that there is a drawing-pin stuck in the wall
of each tyre and that the wheels are in such a position that
these two pins are as close to each other as they could be.

If the front wheel moves forward 42 inches in turning
once and the other moves forward 102 inches in turning
once, how far would Punnish have to push the bicycle
forward in order that these two pins should both once
more occupy the same relative positions? **H**

48 'My father was also a tyreless man. An inventor,' said Punnish, scarcely able to contain his amusement as Pembish tried to look disapproving. 'His bike, if you pardon the term, had metal wheels of circumference 60 and 135 centimetres respectively.'

How far would you have to push this machine forward before both the wheels were again in the same position relative to the road?

49   Punnish has forgotten to wind the Pembish Hall clock. It says 2 pm.

'New-fangled things! All behind-hand and widdershins!' he says and winds it up on the spot. He then drives over to Chronos's house to ask the time. He arrives at 2 pm by Chronos's infallible house-clock.

'I only came to check the time for the Hall clock, sir,' he says when Chronos invites him in. 'But it's obviously all right anyway: that's exactly the same time as it says on our clock back at the Hall. I'd better wander back.'

'Nonsense, man, come in and have a drink. I want to ask your advice about raspberries.'

Punnish leaves when Chronos's clock says 5 pm. He returns to Pembish Hall and to his horror finds the Hall clock now says 5.34.

'Argh! Misbehave while I'm gone, eh? I'll soon set you to rights,' he says, and puts it back to 5.00 again.

The Pembish Hall clock runs, in fact, at precisely the right rate. Is it now ahead of time or behind time and, if so, by how much? **H**

50   Mr Cart has many inventions to his name, mostly to do with some aspect of motion. His latest device is a meter for measuring one's walking-rate. By using this machine, which he has disguised as a walking-stick with a cross-section roughly that of an elephant's foot, one can discover one's rate of walking. He hopes to take the device on a test-walk from his home in Little Twiddings to the Pig and Surgeon, his favourite public house in Much Boshing. He aims to amaze its landlord with this latest device. He is just sneaking down the drive when his wife leans out of the window.

'Where are you off to, Orson?' she trills shrilly.

'Just for a test-walk, dear,' he replies.

'At last,' he thinks, 'I'll be able to arrive dead on opening time.'*

He looks at his binary wrist-watch. 'If I set out now and walk at two miles per hour I shall arrive an hour late. If I set out in an hour and go at five miles per hour I will arrive an hour early.'

Given that opening time is 6 pm in these parts, how far away is the Pig and Surgeon, how fast must he walk if he sets out at once, and what time is it now?

* He means that he hopes to arrive at precisely 6 pm, of course, and not that he will be dead on arrival.

51   Mr Cart met a man with a Russian hat and a briefcase strolling along the road and was able to inform him (thanks to his new rate-meter) that he was walking at two miles per hour.

'You should jog home,' he said. 'That would be three times as fast and twice as healthy.'

'What, *12 miles*?' exclaimed the man, lighting a fat cigar.

'Why ever not? Just think of the time you'd save.'

How much time should the man be thinking of?

52 The Censor was wandering about Little Chiddings with
    calculators and questionnaires in every hand. He came
    across a farmer, who was in a hurry. The Censor asked
    him how many animals he had and of what sort they
    were.

    'Well, since you arsks me like thart . . .' said the farmer,
    pausing to kick the rump of a recalcitrant pig, 'all I has is
    pigs, bar two of 'em, and all I has is horses, bar two of
    'em.'

    'Anything else?' asked the Censor, scribbling away.

    'No, just a cow,' mused the farmer wandering off.

    What had he?

53 After the Censor had unscrambled that one he went off
down the road and met the farmer's brother who had
even less time for busybodies as he was milking his cow.

'I heard about you,' he roared from the barn. 'Well, you
arsked for it. They're all cows but four, all bulls but four.'

'But that won't do . . .' said the Censor.

'Well, the number of horses equals the number of cattle,
not counting any chickens I might have.'

'Oh, do you have any chickens?'

'Maybe I has and maybe I hasn't. Anyway, I haven't anything else.'

How many animals of each type had he?

54 When the Censor asked one woman about her children,
she replied just before closing the door, 'If you multiply
together the ages of all my children the result is 60.
Dividing that by the age of the eldest gives you the sum of
the ages of all three.'

What can be concluded from this?

55 When Pembish first met Miss Grammatica and he asked
her what she did for a living, she replied with a smile that
she was a:

LATHEROSE CHOC.

This puzzled him greatly until he learnt what her first
name was.

What was her occupation? **H**

56 Miss Grammatica then challenged Pembish to find a
    single word in each case for which the following are
    anagrams:

    (i) the classroom
    (ii) mystics in a heap.

57   Miss Grammatica's friend, Miss Bathpale, loves salmon but hates pilchards. She 'simply adores' octopus but 'cannot abide' plaice. She likes trout but not pike. She loves herring but detests kipper.

This much Miss Grammatica knows. But will Miss Bathpale like halibut? **H**

58   A hypochondriac drinks his medicine until there is only a third left in the bottle. He then dilutes the remainder with water until the bottle is two-thirds full. He then decides this might be too weak, so he tops the bottle up with a mixture twice as strong as the original medicine.

Is the resultant mixture stronger or weaker than the mixture he originally began with, and, if so, by how much?

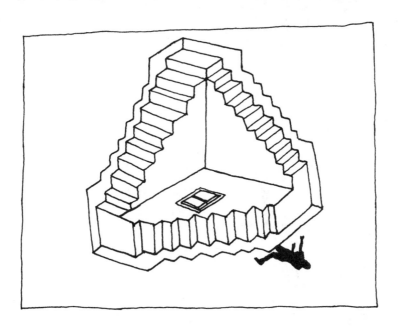

59   A lunatic at the No Rest Home for the Wicked climbs
     stairs by going up five and then down four. He counts one
     for each step he goes up, but neglects to count any steps
     he goes down. All in all, he has counted 45 by the time he
     reaches the top landing.

     How many steps are there?

60 'If it takes 1½ men 1½ days,' says Punnish, strutting about in imitation of his master, 'to pot 1½ geraniums in 1½ pots, how many will 2½ men pot in 6 days?'

He is rather shocked to hear Pembish answering this rhetorical question from within the greenhouse.

What, incidentally, is the answer?

61   Plantpott-Smythe, as ever, is trying to doze down at The Old India when his reveries are again interrupted, this time by the following colloquy from somewhere beyond the potted palm:

A says, 'My dear boy, I am six times as old as you were when I was as old as you are.'

B replies, 'Ah yes, but that was exactly two years after you were six times as old as I was.'

How old are the interlocutors? **H**

62   To catch the Christmas mail Professor Puttylump sprints
to the Post Office at six miles per hour. He turns round as
soon as he arrives and immediately sets out for home at a
leisurely two miles per hour. As he reaches his house he
bumps into the irrepressible Mr Cart with his elephanto-
podean odometer.

'Do you know,' calls Mr Cart loudly, 'what my rate-meter
gives for your overall average speed?'

'Yes,' snaps Puttylump, escaping into the sanctuary of his
own driveway. Cart doesn't hear the answer as he had his
headphones on.

What is it?   **H**

63   Dr Michael Robe of the Department of Immaterial Science is conducting a demonstration for his students.

'If I put an amoeba in this jar it will divide into two in a day and each resulting amoeba will also divide into two in a day and so on. In fact, this jar will be full of amoebas in 12 days. However, as we are close to the end of term, I will start our experiment off not with one amoeba, but with twice as many. How many days will that save us, eh Ponsonby*?'

What should Ponsonby have answered?

64 Pembish has a selection of identical ping-pong balls. He
wishes to stick them all together but runs out of superglue
just as he has finished coating the first one.

What is the largest number of ping-pong balls he can
make into a cluster by sticking the remaining unsticky
balls to the sticky one?

65 Miss Highwater (Helen to her friends) drives up from Oxford to London. On arrival in London, she discovers that her average speed for the journey has been 30 miles per hour. On the way back, she is determined, in spite of the obstacles placed in her path by the highway engineers to make up for lost time and make her overall average speed for the whole journey 60 miles per hour.

How fast must she travel on the way back up to Oxford in order to do this? **H**

66 Professor Mozzarella is being visited by his seven nephews and is giving them tea. He brings out a beautiful round fruit-cake. What is the minimum number of cuts he need make in order that he and his nephews should all have an equal share of the cake?

67 The houses in Kitten Mews are all of the same size and are
    uniformly spaced so that each and every house is directly
    opposite a corresponding one on the other side of the
    street. Moreover, the houses are numbered *boustrophedon**,
    i.e. 1, 2, 3, etc., up one side and then back again along the
    other.

    The postman notices as he delivers a letter to number 37
    that the house directly opposite it is number 64.

    How many houses are there in the street? **H**

* According to Szklowski, this word comes from the Greek and means
'as the ox turns'. In ploughing a field, the ox would go the length of the
field and then come back. Streets are numbered *boustrophedon* if the
house numbering increases along one side and then continues back
along the other.

68 'Well, I was proceeding down Lettsby Avenue,' said PC Klepto, 'and had just turned into Silent Mews.'

'And what time was this?' asked Q C Casey, QC.

'Well I don't remember, but the hour hand and the minute hand were *exactly* on minute-divisions of the clock-face and the minute hand was *exactly* 13 minute-divisions ahead of the hour hand.'

Luckily Dr Chronos was in the court. What time does he suggest the recorder record? **H**

69   Mr Metal was a music lover. His only recording of Horace
      Toccato's *Moonshine Sonata* was cut neatly into two halves
      by his rather difficult son, Rocco. With a sigh Mr Metal
      reached for the superglue and stuck the two pieces
      together again, being careful to align the grooves under a
      magnifying glass.

      'There,' he said. 'Good as new!' But when he looked
      more closely at the disc he found that he had stuck the
      halves together the wrong way round, so that each face of
      the record now had half the grooves belonging to side A
      and half those belonging to side B.

      If he had put the record on the turntable, would the
      needle have followed the groove all the way to the end of
      that side?

      (The grooves are all of the same width and are of equal
      number on each side.)

70　Mr Buttermilk is so convinced that his poems will be plagiarised if he leaves them lying around that he uses all sorts of ingenious codes to conceal their true value from the marauding eye. One such trick is to merge the words of the title in such a way that the letters of each individual word of the title still occur in the right order but the words are merged into one long one.

He was just about to send off one of his many odes to the publishers when he realised he had not unscrambled the title. He knew it was just two words, but as he confronted the piece of paper with:

PFLROETWTEYR

written on it, his heart sank.

Can you help him if he lets you?

71 When Professor Tringle's triplets were born she nick-
    named them A, B and C, and, so as not to confuse them,
    had their clothes monogrammed with these letters so that
    they were identifiable at a glance.

    One day, A said to the brother wearing the letter B, 'Do
    you realise, we are all wearing the wrong letters today?'

    Who was wearing which letter?

72 A cockerel perches on the ridge of a roof, the sides of
which slope down at angles of 30 degrees and 45 degrees
to the horizontal respectively. If the cockerel lays an egg,
will the egg roll down the side with the steep slope or the
side with the gentler slope?

73 When Mr Drubchifel returned from a hard day at The
    Garlic Press, where he had been supervising the writing
    of a dictionary, his son challenged him facetiously to find
    an English word in which the vowels a, e, i, o and u and
    the half-vowel y all appear in the right order. His father
    mentioned the problem to Mr Striker, who gave up
    smoking several times while looking for an answer.

    What might it have been? **H**

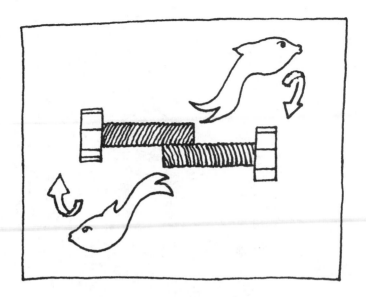

74   Professor Didipotamus, whose left hand very often
      doesn't know what his right hand is doing, is absent-
      mindedly fiddling with two bolts (both with right-hand
      threads) as he talks to a fish. If he turns them in opposite
      directions with their grooves interlocking, as shown
      below, will the heads move closer together, further apart
      or keep the same distance from each other?   **H**

75 Professor Didipotamus was walking up Hochstrasse when he chanced to put his hand in his pocket.

'Oh no,' he thought, 'I've left my pipe at my lodgings. I wonder what else I've forgotten. Oh, yes,' he said to himself as his hand encountered a full tin of tobacco. 'Tobacco.'

He went into Yorvas's, where he bought a pipe and some tobacco. This came to £11, the pipe costing £10 more than the tobacco.

'That's very odd,' thought Didipotamus as he put the new pipe with an almost identical one he had just found in his jacket pocket, and then tried to understand why he should have two tins of tobacco floating around in his pocket. 'That tobacco was cheap. . . .'

How much had it in fact cost him? **H**

76 A deaf spy is sent to spy on an airfield. He takes a room in
    the boarding house of Mrs Oldham. Every now and then,
    and at random, he makes an excuse to go up to his attic
    room in order to watch the aerodrome with his opera
    glasses until he sees an aeroplane. He then immediately
    makes a note of this in his report and goes back down-
    stairs.

Back in Oblivia, Funkov goes through the spy's report. 'It
is worse than useless,' he says. 'We already know that
every single hour, day and night, exactly one plane lands,
refuels and leaves in a perfectly regular fashion. And yet
this report states that he finds *11* times as many planes
landing as taking off.'

'Hm,' says his colleague, Khatzov. 'That makes sense. We
can get *some* useful information out of it.'

What information can be had from these facts? **H**

77 It is the first anniversary of the formation of the Zircon zargo team. Each player, being a clone, secretly buys all the other players a ticket to *Quagmoth*, a Revolutionary Ballet of the Spheres, except for the goalkeeper who, being forgetful, doesn't buy any. As a result, 1,183 dinglies are spent.

How many men are there in a zargo team and how much are the tickets? **H**

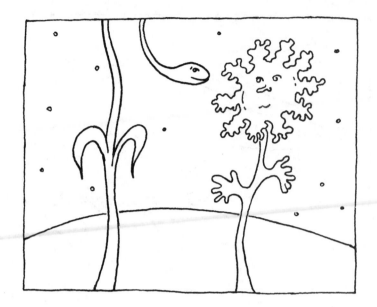

78 There are two types of Zirconian fritillary: the White and
    the Snakeshead. Both grow to a height of 55 zonks. The
    White, however, grows at a rate of one zonk in the first
    tink, two zonks in the second tink, three zonks in the
    third tink, etc. The Snakeshead variety grows in such a
    way that its height increases by three zonks in the first
    two tinks, by six zonks in the second two tinks, nine
    zonks in the third two tinks, etc. They both germinate
    (from zero height) at the same time.

    Which of the two will be fully grown first?

79 Mr Striker smokes far too much. He has given up the habit almost as many times as he has taken it up again. When given a packet of 20 most excellent Egyptian cigarettes he cannot resist them. His friends have prevailed upon him to make some concession to health and so he smokes only a third of each cigarette, discarding the remaining two-thirds. But, having finished the packet, he rather shamefacedly makes whole cigarettes out of the stubs and begins again, that is smoking a third of each reconstituted cigarette. He continues this process until he can get no more whole cigarettes out of the stub ends.

At this point his wife comes in and exclaims, 'Oh Oscar, you've been smoking again!'

'Only one, dear,' he says, pointing at the stub in the ashtray with a pleading expression.

'Oscar, you're *almost* intolerable!' she says, walking out of the room.

How many smokes has he had and how many cigarettes has he smoked up?

80 Mr Striker is walking home across the parks. It is a walk
which takes exactly two cigarettes. In his cigarette case he
has two Craven Doodahs and a pair of El-Rashids (which
he prefers).

What are the chances of his smoking two El-Rashids in
such a walk if he withdraws cigarettes randomly from the
case?

As night fell, the man rose from his chair, resolving to defer the journey to the pyrgos in the far-off land. 'I shall set out tomorrow, if at all,' he said, 'and even if I never go, it is better to have travelled in an armchair than never to have travelled at all.'

6 Since clones are alike, they each must have bought exactly the same.

10 Think of the electricity bill.

11 If there was no water in the glass, the ice cube would fall to the bottom. It must be the water which supports it. The buoyancy of the water must just balance the weight of the ice cube.

12 Remember freezing point is 0°C or 32°F and boiling point is 100°C or 212°F. So a change of temperature of 180° on the Fahrenheit scale corresponds to a change of 100° on the Centigrade scale. The temperature Cryogenes refers to must be below freezing point.

13 The answer is not 2013.

15 To raise a number to a power means to multiply it by itself that many times. Thus:

   2 to the power 3, or $2^3 = 2 \times 2 \times 2 = 8$.
   3 to the power 2, or $3^2 = 3 \times 3 = 9$.

16 If the swimmer swims with the tide, his net speed will be his speed in still water added to the speed of the moving water. If he swims against the tide, his net speed will be the difference between his speed in still water and the speed of the moving water.

20 The numerator is the number on the top of the fraction and the denominator is the one on the bottom. Thus in the fraction $\frac{7}{29}$, 7 is the numerator and 29 is the denominator.

24 It wasn't a BOX, as Mr Juniper-Berry was quick to point out. It had a smooth grey trunk, spreading branches, and dark green leaves.

26 Adding any two-digit number to the number formed by reversing the order of the digits of the original number produces a number which is equal to 11 times the sum of the digits of the original number.

   For example, adding 59 to 95 gives 154 and this is equal to 11×14 (where $14 = 5 + 9$).

27 A prime number is an integer (whole number) which has no other factors besides itself and one. A factor is an integer which divides into a number a whole number of times.

For example, 2, 3, 4 and 6 are all factors of 12, but 5 is not, because it will not go into 12 a whole number of times.

Fifteen is not a prime number because it has factors 3 and 5. But 7 is a prime number because it has no other factors besides 7 and 1.

A perfect square is a number made from multiplying an integer by itself. Thus 16 is a perfect square because it equals 4×4.

See also hint 26.

30 Telephonopoulos doesn't rule out the use of some of the digits as powers. For example, one could use up the digits 2 and 6 in writing 6^2 (which stands for 6×6, i.e. 36), which is exactly what Stars did.

32 Try leaving Szklowski out of the reckoning.

36 In the first part, as Chronos soon discovered, the squares do not all have to be the same size. In the second part, Striker forgot to mention that some glue might come in handy.

37 An equilateral triangle is a triangle with all its sides the same length.

Using a little glue would make this problem a little easier.

38 In each of the two preceding puzzles Striker has taken pains to point out that the matches must not be broken or overlap (they must only touch at the ends). In this puzzle he says that the matches must not be broken, but he doesn't mention their overlapping.

39 Notice that Chronos's clock has the same number of hours on it as there are days in the week. That being the case and given that Chronos takes the week as starting on midnight on Sunday, there is something special about midday on Thursday.

40 See hint 39.

43 If you prefer an algebraic approach, put A's age as a and B's age as a + x. In x years' time A will be the age that B is now and x years ago B was the age A is now.

If you prefer trial and error it might help to know that both A and B are less than 10 years old.

44 Let A's age be x. Then B's age is 3x. Then B's reply means that his age now (3x) is twice what A's will be in 15 years' time (x + 15).

45 It might help to know that the surface area of a sphere is four times the area of a circle of the same radius.

47 The front wheel will revolve a whole number of times if 42 inches divides a whole number of times into the distance the wheel moves forward.

49 How long is it between the two times that Punnish remonstrates with the Pembish Hall Clock?

55 Miss Grammatica's first name is Anna.

57 Miss Bathpale (or Miss Alphabet, as Miss Grammatica prefers to call her) orders her fish according to how it is spelt on the menu.

If it were not for the last example, Miss Grammatica might well have thought that her friend did not like fish with Is in.

61 It is very difficult to doze off with a conundrum of this calibre running through one's mind. Old 'Plantpott' determined, therefore, to reach a solution as quickly as possible, and reasoned as follows:

The speakers refer to three distinct points in time. At the earliest of these A was six times as old as B. If B had been one year old then, A would have been six years old. In that case, two years later A would have been eight years old and B would have been three years old. So now, when B is as old as A was then, i.e. eight, A would be 13. But 13 is not 6 × 3. So B cannot have been one year old at the earliest of the times mentioned by the speakers.

'Plantpott' then tried another number for B's age at the earliest of the times referred to, and in this way soon reached a solution.

62 The average speed for a journey is the total distance travelled divided by the time it took. Note that the average speed cannot be obtained just by finding the average of the two speeds involved.

65 How long would the round trip take if Miss Highwater were to succeed in her driving ambition?

67 Think about the numbers of opposing houses.

68 The hour hand falls on an exact minute division every fifth of an hour.

73 For one possible solution re-read No. 73.

74 Imagine that one of the bolts is *turned* into a nut. . . .

75 The tobacco did not cost £1.

76 As Khatzov remarked to his colleague: 'If the hourly plane spent a very, very short time on the ground before taking off again, which would our man be more likely to see first if he waited – a plane landing, or a plane taking off?

77 1183 dinglies are spent in all. The dingly is the smallest unit of Zirconian currency. So each ticket cost a whole number of dinglies.

In a far-off land, a man stood at the window of his pyrgos surveying the world below and waiting for a letter bearing an answer. . . .

2 B is not only a man, but also a priest.

4 His house is at the North Pole. Thus all four walls face south. As for the sunbathing, I *did* say he was an eccentric. **A**

6 As clones are identical, one can be sure that they each bought exactly the same. Now 10 dongs equals 110 dinglies, so that, as they spent 10 dongs and 8 dinglies, 118 dinglies were spent in all.

Since each clone had to spend a whole number of dinglies (as these are the smallest unit of currency) and there was a whole number of clones, we need to find two whole numbers which when multiplied together give 118. The only two such numbers are 2 and 59. Thus there were either 2 clones who spent 59 dinglies each, or 59 clones who spent 2 dinglies each. From the wording we know there were more than 2 clones. So that, unfortunately for the washer-upper, there must have been a party of 59 clones who spent only 2 dinglies each. **A**

8 The most the fly can hope to walk without retracing her steps is nine centimetres. One possible path is as shown in Fig. 1. Any other path covers nine centimetres or less.

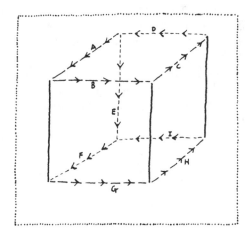

10   Because the room would heat up.

When the refrigerator door is open, heat from the room enters it and the motor runs in an attempt to maintain the low temperature of the inside. The device works by removing heat from the ice-box and expelling it into the room and, in order to do this, it has to consume electrical power. This also ends up as heat which is expelled into the room. In other words, the refrigerator expels more heat into the room than it removes from the ice-box, the discrepancy being due to the electrical power being consumed. The room, therefore, heats up.

12   The temperature was –40°C or –40°F. This is the only temperature which has the same numerical value on both scales.   **A**

14   He had three apples. For if Moore were to have had 1½ times as many apples as he in fact had, he would have had what he in fact had plus 1½ apples. So 1½ apples represents half of what he had. He must, therefore, have had three apples.

16   It would take him three minutes to swim there and back.

Swimming against the tide, his speed is equal to that of the tide (though in the opposite direction). In still water it is twice the speed of the tide. Swimming with the tide, it is three times the speed of the tide. If we call the time it takes to swim the distance between shore and buoy when swimming against the tide 1 yonk, then with the tide it will take ⅓ yonk and in still water ½ yonk. To swim there and back therefore takes 1 yonk in still water and ⁴⁄₃ yonk when there is a tide (since it takes 1 yonk for the part of the swim that is against the tide, and ⅓ yonk for the part of the swim that is with the tide). This is ⅓ as long again as the time taken to do the round trip in still water. Since it takes four minutes when there is a tide, it must take three minutes when there is no tide.

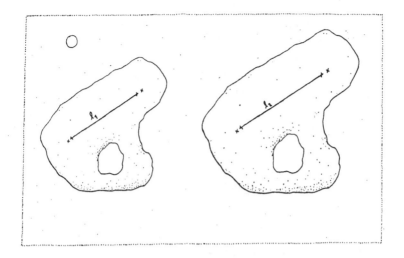

18 When a piece of metal is heated or is cooled it expands or contracts uniformly*. The effect is just the same as if the whole body were scaled up or scaled down. So any hole in the metal would expand or contract in proportion with the bulk of the metal. The iron washer would expand as would the hole in it and the jumblium washer and its hole would contract.

20 The number that must be added to the top and bottom of ¼ to yield ⅔ is 5. For, adding 5 to the numerator and denominator of ¼ gives ⁶⁄₉, which is the same as ⅔. **A**

22 The answer is ox. *Zo* (or *dzo*, or *zho*), by the way, is a Himalayan ox. An *ai* is a three-toed sloth. *Em* and *en* are units of length in printing and *mu* is the letter of the Greek alphabet corresponding to *m*.

24 Stars looked out of the window and saw a BEECH tree. It had always been there but he had just never really noticed it before.

The letters B, C, D, E, H, I, K, O and X all retain their identity when turned upside down and viewed in a mirror. All the other letters cease to represent letters at all except for M which becomes W and W which becomes M. Any word made from the letters listed above will read the same

---

* (Provided that it is free to expand or contract and is not constrained in any way.)

when viewed inverted in a mirror. For example: CHECK, BOX, DICE, DECK, COOKBOOK (as in the illustration), etc.

Stars realised, on reflection, that the undergraduette's name also had this special sort of symmetry. What was her name? **A**

26 She was 19 years old. This can be seen easily by drawing up a table of ages.

Age	Result	Largest factor less than 11
10	11	1
11	22	2
12	33	3
13	44	4
14	55	5
15	66	6
16	77	7
17	88	8
18	99	9
19	110	10
20	22	2
21	33	3

and so on.

In the first column are possible ages. The result of reversing the digits and adding this to the original number appears in the second column. In the final column are the largest numbers less than 11 which will divide exactly into the numbers in the second column. The only age for which this number is 10 is seen to be 19. **A**

28 There are many ways. For example,

$$0 + 1 + 2 + 3 + 4 + 5 + 6 + 7 + (8 \times 9) = 100$$

Or,

$$
\begin{array}{r}
0 \\
17 \\
36 \\
+ \ 45 \\
\hline
= \ 98 \\
+ \ 2 \\
\hline
= 100
\end{array}
$$

30 It is in fact impossible to produce the number 100 by adding together single or two-digit numbers using all the digits from 0 to 9 once and once only. It is, however, possible to produce the number 100 by using addition signs only if we resort to the trick of using the digit 2 as the sign for 'squared':

$$0 + 1 + 4 + 5 + 7 + 8 + 9 + 30 + 6^2 = 100$$

in which 6^2 stands for $6 \times 6 = 36$. **A**

32 Ten people had coffee, milk and sugar.

Of the 13 people having coffee, 12 had milk. Therefore only 1 person had no milk in his coffee. This was Szklowski (by his own admission). He had no sugar in it either.

Now, consider all those taking sugar. These must have consisted of two groups: those having sugar and milk and those having sugar but no milk. But only one person had no milk and he also had no sugar. Therefore there were no people who had sugar but did not have milk. Thus everyone who had sugar also had milk. So there were 10 people who had all three.

34 It was 2.10 and 55 seconds approximately.

In 12 hours, the little hand goes round the clockface once and the big hand 12 times. The big hand thus overtakes the little hand 11 times in the course of 12 hours, at intervals of $^{12}/_{11}$ hours. That is, every 1 hour, 5 minutes and 27.3 seconds (approximately). As it was around two o'clock and the hands were touching, it must have been the second time the hands coincided after midday, and therefore 2×1 hour, 5 minutes and 27.3 seconds after midday, i.e. at 2.10 and 55 seconds (approximately).

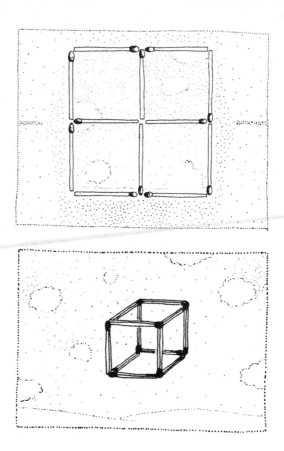

36 Chronos first laid out the matches as in Fig. 3.

The larger square forms the fifth square.

To turn these matches into six squares Chronos had to glue them into a cubical network as shown in Fig. 4. This has twelve edges and six square faces.

38 He could write it in Roman numerals: XII.

40 Given that at noon on Thursday Chronos's clock would say seven o'clock (see answer to puzzle 39), it should have said 1 o'clock at 1 p.m. that afternoon. Thus it stopped either at one p.m. or at any multiple of seven hours previous to that. Chronos tells us that it stopped in the morning so it must have stopped seven hours before at 6 a.m.

42 The girl is his niece. Cruddington's mother's only daughter is *his* sister. Thus Cruddington is claiming that his sister is the girl's mother, or, in other words, that he is her uncle.

44 A is 30 years old and B is 90.

To prove this, let A's age be x and B's age will therefore be $3x$. B's age ($3x$) is twice what A's will be in 15 years' time (i.e. $x + 15$). This gives the equation:

$$3x = 2(x + 15)$$
$$3x = 2x + 30$$
$$\text{So,} \quad x = 30$$

Therefore A is 30 and B is 90.

46 The number of cannonballs in a square layer can be worked out by multiplying the number of balls along one edge by itself. Thus the number of cannonballs in a layer with an even number of balls along its edge is even and the number of balls in a layer with an odd number of cannonballs along its edge is odd, simply because, as Pembish knew, an even number times an even number is always even and an odd number times an odd number is odd.

In a pyramid of 30 layers of the kind described, there are 15 layers containing an even number of cannonballs and 15 containing an odd number. The 15 even layers will yield an even number, and the 15 odd layers an odd number. When these two numbers are added together this produces an odd number since an odd number and an even, when added, yield an odd number. Therefore, there is an odd number of cannonballs in the heap and so it cannot be split into two equal piles. **A**

48 80 centimetres. (See answer to puzzle 47.)

50 The Pig and Surgeon is 10 miles away and he must walk at
2½ miles per hour to get there at opening time.

The time now is 2 pm.

Let the distance be x and the time now T. If he leaves now
and walks at two miles per hour he will arrive an hour late,
i.e. at 7 p.m. Therefore the time taken in hours will be
$(7 - T)$. As his speed is two miles per hour, the distance he
walks in this time will be: $x = 2(7 - T)$.

If he sets out in an hour and walks at five miles per hour he
will arrive an hour early. That is, he will spend, all in all,
three hours less in travelling there, i.e. $(4 - T)$ hours. In
each hour he will walk five miles, so the distance he will
walk will be: $x = 5(4 - T)$.

By equating these two expressions we find that:
$14 - 2T = 20 - 5T$

Adding $5T$ to each side gives: $14 + 3T = 20$. Subtracting 14
from each side gives: $3T = 6$. So $T = 2$. That is, it is now two
o'clock. Thus, if he leaves now and walks at two miles per
hour, he will walk for five hours at two miles per hour in
order to arrive at the pub at seven o'clock. The pub must
therefore be 10 miles away. If he leaves now he has to walk
10 miles in four hours, so he must walk at 2½ miles per
hour.

52 He has a pig, a cow and a horse.

Let the number of pigs be p and the number of horses be h. He has one cow. We are told the 'non-pigs' are two in number. One of these is a cow, so the other must be a horse. He has, therefore, one cow and one horse. The number of 'non-horses' is two and one of these is a cow, so the other must be a pig.

54 Her children are three, four and five years old.

The possible combinations of three whole numbers which give 60 on multiplying are:

$1 \times 1 \times 60$	$1 \times 6 \times 10$
$1 \times 2 \times 30$	$2 \times 2 \times 15$
$1 \times 3 \times 20$	$2 \times 3 \times 10$
$1 \times 4 \times 15$	$2 \times 5 \times 6$
$1 \times 5 \times 12$	$3 \times 4 \times 5$

The only combination which adds together to give the same number as one gets from dividing 60 by the largest number is the last, so her children are three, four and five years old.

56 (i) Schoolmaster
    (ii) Metaphysicians

58 He ends up with a mixture which is of the same strength as the mixture he originally started with.

If the original mixture in the bottle contained $3x$ grams of active substance in water, then, when he has drunk two-thirds of the bottle, there will be x grams of active substance left in it. After adding a third of a bottle of water we still have x grams of active ingredient in the bottle, which is now two-thirds full of mixture. The mixture he then adds to the bottle has twice the strength of the original and so contains $6x$ grams of active substance in a bottle the same size as the original. Thus, a third of a bottle the size of the original one but containing a substance of double strength will contain $2x$ grams, when the medicine bottle is topped up, then, $2x$ grams is added to the x grams already there. So there will again be $3x$ grams of active substance in it. Whatever is not active substance is water, and since the two together make the bottle full again, we have the same amount of active substance in the same amount of water, i.e. the same strength of mixture as he originally began with.

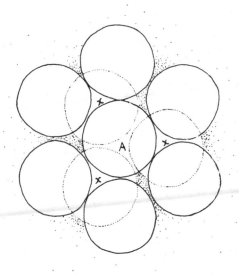

60 If it takes 1½ men 1½ days to pot 1½ geraniums, ½ a man
will pot ½ a geranium in that time. Thus one man will pot
one geranium in 1½ days. In six days, one man will pot
four geraniums and 1½ will pot six. So, putting them
together, 2½ men will pot 10 geraniums (in 10 pots).

62 Puttylump's overall average speed was three miles per
hour.

If the distance to the post box is L miles, and if A is the time
taken on the way there, since he was walking at six miles
per hour, $A = L/6$. Similarly, if B is the time he takes to
come back, $B = L/2$, since he was travelling at two miles per
hour. So the total time taken is: $A + B$; or, $L/6 + L/2$; or,
$2L/3$. Therefore the average speed is $2L$ divided by $2L/3$,
which is three miles per hour.

64 The answer is 13.

If one arranges the ping-pong balls on a flat surface such as
a table-top exactly six can be placed around the central ball
A, as in Fig. 6. Three can be placed in contact with A in the
positions marked X in the plane above A and, in a similar
way, three others can be placed in similar positions in the
plane below. Thus 12 can be made to touch the centre ball
and the cluster will contain 13 balls altogether. **A**

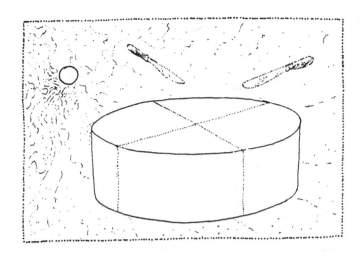

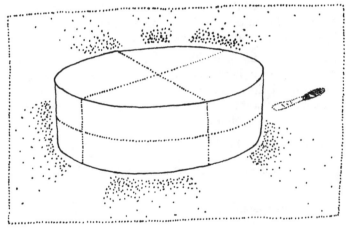

66 There are eight people. So the minimum number of cuts
    required is three: two in the vertical plane (as in Fig. 7): and
    one in the horizontal plane dividing the cake into two equal
    pieces (as in Fig. 8), which gives eight pieces in all:

68   The time was 4.36 precisely.

In one hour, the hour hand traverses five minute-divisions. So every fifth of an hour, that is every 12 minutes, it will be exactly on a minute-division. Thus it is always exactly on a minute-division on every hour, and also 12 minutes, 24 minutes, 36 minutes and 48 minutes past every hour. If the time was on the hour, the minute hand would be on 12 and the hour hand on one of the hour-divisions and so the former could *not* be 13 minute-divisions ahead of the hour hand. If the time was 24 minutes after an hour, the hour hand would have to be on the 11 minute-division. It would then be on the minute-division after the second hour-division, but this would correspond to $2\frac{1}{5}$ hours, that is 2.12, and not 2.24. If it were 48 minutes past an hour, the hour hand would have to be on the 35th minute-division, which corresponds to the seventh hour-division. So the hour hand would be on 7 and the minute hand could not be on the 48 minute-division.

On the other hand, as Chronos pointed out, if it were 36 minutes past an hour, the hour hand, being 13 minute-divisions behind, would be on the 23 minute-division, which corresponds to $4\frac{3}{5}$ hour-divisions. But $\frac{3}{5}$ of an hour is 36 minutes, so that must have been the time.   **A**

70   Pretty Flower.

72   The answer is yes: it will roll down one side or the other.   **A**

74   They move towards each other.   **A**

76   If the plane takes x minutes to refuel and take off again, the fraction of the hour during which it is on the ground is $\frac{x}{60}$. If the spy goes up to his room during this time, he will next see a plane taking off. If he arrives outside this fraction of the hour, the next event he will observe will be a plane landing. But the chances of his getting to the window at a time when the plane is on the ground are $\frac{x}{60}$. Since, on average, out of every 12 planes he sees only one taking off, his chances of observing a take-off are $\frac{1}{12}$. This must equal $\frac{x}{60}$. Therefore, $\frac{1}{12} = \frac{x}{60}$, so that $x = 5$. Thus the plane takes five minutes to refuel and take off again.

78 The increments at the end of each tink are shown in the table:

	White	Snakeshead
1st	1	—
2nd	2	3
3rd	3	—
4th	4	6
5th	5	—
6th	6	9
7th	7	—
8th	8	12
9th	9	—
10th	10	15

The heights are thus:

1st	1	—
2nd	3	3
3rd	6	—
4th	10	9
5th	15	—
6th	21	18
7th	28	—
8th	36	30
9th	45	—
10th	55	45

Thus the White arrives at its full height first, after 10 tinks.

80 His chances are one in six.

Let the cigarettes be labelled *E1*, *E2*, *C1* and *C2*. The possible choices are:

E1/C1	E1/C2	E1/E2
E2/C1	E2/C2	E2/E1
C1/C2	C1/E1	C1/E2
C2/C1	C2/E1	C2/E1

Of these 12 possible ways only two are favourable. So his chances are a sixth.

Alternatively, consider the chances of withdrawing an El-Rashid the first time: this is ½. This then leaves two Cravens and one El-Rashid. The chance of withdrawing the next El-Rashid are ⅓. The chances of both these happening in the same walk is the product of these two, namely ⅙.

1   The phrase 'the brother of X's brother's sister' could refer to X or to X's brother. Thus the speaker is saying either that Cruddington is the girl's uncle or that his brother is. In the first case the girl is his niece. In the second she is his niece or his daughter. But Cruddington has no children. So the speaker is referring to Cruddington's niece.

3   One of them is mistaken or lying.

5   Pembish's second house has windows in the east side only.

If you think Pembish is eccentric, you should see the house of his mathematician colleague, Hermann Klaus, who used a large Klein bottle discarded by the roadside as his phrontisterion.* (A Klein bottle may be made by passing the neck of a bottle through its side. The resultant body has neither an inside nor an outside. Thus Klaus was able to be 'in' and 'out' at one and the same time and yet be neither, a fact which has proved useful in discouraging unwelcome visitors and has proved instrumental in curing him of his *Klaus*trophobia.) Mr Buttermilk has immortalised him in the following lines:

> A mad mathematician named Klaus
> Lived in a Klein-Bottlehaus.
> When one knocked at his door,
> One just couldn't be sure
> If he'd say 'komm herein' or 'heraus'.

* phrontisterion: a study or room for thinking in

7 The boy was obviously bright for his age, even if he does seem to refer to his uncle as 'Da'.

After the first bounce, the ball rises to a height of half a metre and then falls the same distance. Thus it travels one metre between the first and second bounce. It then bounces up a quarter metre and falls just as far, totalling half a metre between the second and third bounce. So, counting the height from which the ball fell initially (i.e. one metre), the total distance travelled will be:

$$1 + (1 + \tfrac{1}{2} + \tfrac{1}{4} + \tfrac{1}{8} + \ldots)$$

i.e. three metres. **A**

9 It will take 12 minutes for the bath to fill.

The cold tap delivers a bathload of water in three minutes and the hot one in four minutes. In 12 minutes therefore the cold would fill four baths and the hot would fill three baths. So in 12 minutes the two taps together would fill seven baths. The plughole empties six baths in 12 minutes so, with both taps running and the plughole open, one bath will fill in 12 minutes. **A**

11 No, he is wrong. As the ice melts there will be no change in the level of the water. **A**

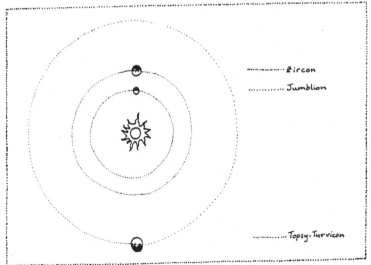

13 They will next lie in a straight line in six years' time in 2007, when they will have the configuration shown in Fig. 10. Topsy-Turvicon ends up on the opposite side of Brillo from the other two planets, which is why it was so christened by Dr Stars. (Jumblion, by the way, is a planet composed almost entirely of the metal jumblium, the bounciest of all substances.)

107

15 The number of hens and the number of eggs they lay cannot be the same or the farmer would not have remarked on the coincidence of the matter. So we must look for two different numbers which will satisfy the farmer's stipulation. Now, if we happen to know that the only numbers which fulfill this are 2 and 4, i.e. $2^4 = 4^2$, then our troubles are over. So the farmer had either four hens laying two eggs each, or two hens laying four eggs, and so had eight eggs per day in all. As the farmer said it would be cheaper from the point of view of feeding them if he could swap round the number of hens and the number of eggs, he must have four hens laying two eggs each. **A**

17 Neither. If both are worth their weight in gold, then a kilogram of zolots and a kilogram of five-zolot pieces are both *worth* the same since they *weigh* the same. **A**

19 When the number of cows is increased from three to four the provender rises by one bale of hay. Each cow is identical and so needs exactly the same amount of food. One bale of hay, or its equivalent in turnips, is the allowance per cow. If three cows need one bale of hay and seven turnips, and since one more cow is adequately provided for by the additional bale of hay, seven turnips will suffice for two cows. Therefore six cows would require 21 turnips in the absence of hay.

21 Knightsbridge (of which 'Bithkrieg Gdns' in the illustration is an anagram). **A**

23 Of the 26 letters of the alphabet, the only ones which, when printed in block capitals, appear unchanged when held up sideways to a mirror are: A, H, I, M, O, T, U, V, W, X and Y

Any word made up solely of these letters down the page will remain unchanged by reflection in a mirror: e.g. WHAT, MOAT, AXIOM, MOUTH, TOMATO, OATH, ATOM, WHIT, MAXIM, MOTH, MYTH, WAX, TAUT, HIT, HOT, TOY, WHIM, VOMIT, TOW, VOW, MAW, THAT, VAT, WAVY, HAT, YAM, WAY, WITH, HAY, WAIT, OX, AT, HAM, HOAX, TAXI, HAITI, TAHITI, etc.

Incidentally, Stars's brother has a name (not appearing in the above list) with this special sort of reflection symmetry. What is his brother's name? **A**

25 QUEUE (a word inspired, no doubt, by the wait).

27 Stars is 65 years old, but he wished that he was nine years younger.

If his age is written AB, this stands for A tens and B units, i.e. $10A + B$ years. Reversing the digits of his age produces BA, which stands for B tens and A units, i.e. $10B + A$. Adding these together we get: $11A + 11B = 11(A + B)$. Now, since A and B are digits, $(A + B)$ must be less than 18, since A and B are both equal to or less than 9. We therefore want a number between 2 and 18 which when multiplied by 11 gives a perfect square. The only possibility is if $(A + B) = 11$. The ages for which the sum of the digits is 11 are:

29, 38, 47, 56, 65, 74, 83, and 92.

We know his age is odd and not prime. As 29, 47 and 83 are all prime numbers, he must therefore be 65.

Now Stars wishes that his age, as well as producing a perfect square, were also divisible by 4, as it once had been. The only numbers in the list above which are divisible by 4 are 56 and 92. But, if he is 65, he has never been 92 and thus can only wish to be 56, i.e. nine years younger. **A**

29 Zero. Multiplying anything by zero yields zero. Stars made the mistake of doing the addition first. No wonder he felt sheepish: all that work for nothing! **A**

31 The digit 0 appears 11 times, the digit 1 appears 21 times. All the others appear 20 times each. **A**

33 He made one coffee with cream and sugar, one with cream and rum, and one with sugar and rum.

35 If he chooses the first sock at random there will be seven socks left in the drawer. Only one of these will be the corresponding one. Therefore he has a one in seven chance of picking the right one. If he chooses his socks at random like this, he will wear a matching pair of socks on average only one day a week. **A**

37 By making a regular tetrahedron (as hinted at in the drawing accompanying the puzzle):

39 5.30 pm.

The hour hand of a 12-hour clock goes round the clock-face twice in a 24-hour day and therefore 14 times in a week. There are 168 hours in a week; so midway through the week, if the week starts at midnight Sunday, is 84 hours later, i.e. midday Thursday. In 84 hours, the seven-hour clock will have performed exactly 12 cycles. Thus its hands will be in coincidence at noon on Thursday. At noon on Thursday, as at midnight Sunday, Chronos's clock will read seven o'clock. At 5.30 pm (by the 12-hour clock) on Thursday afternoon, just 5½ hours later, the seven-hour clock will thus say 5.30 pm also.

41 He had been reading it upside down.

43 A is five and B is seven. **A**

45 He would require five more tins.

The surface area of a sphere of radius R is four times the area of a circle of the same radius. Cutting a sphere in half produces two such circles and so adds half its surface area again. Thus if 10 tins of paint were required for the spheres, an extra five tins will be required if the spheres are cut in half.

47 We need to find the smallest distance into which both 42 inches and 102 inches will both divide exactly. Let this distance be x. Now this means that x must be divisible by both 42 and 102. Since $42 = 7 \times 6$, x must also be divisible by 7 and 6. Similarly, $102 = 17 \times 6$, so x must be divisible by 17 and 6. We require the smallest number, then, which is divisible by 6, 7 and 17:

$$6 \times 7 \times 17 = 714 \text{ inches}$$

So, the bicycle will have to move forward 59 feet and 6 inches. **A**

49 The Pembish Hall clock was now 17 minutes slow. Punnish stays three hours at Chronos's. Suppose the journey from Pembish Hall to Chronos's house took time t. He thus arrives back at Pembish Hall three hours plus $2t$ after setting out. But the clock has moved on from 2.00 to 5.34, so that $2t$ must equal 34 minutes. That is, the journey must have taken 17 minutes each way. Thus the correct time when he arrived home was 5.17. Punnish, in setting Pembish's clock at 5.00, has therefore made it 17 minutes slow. **A**

51 Walking 12 miles at two miles per hour takes six hours. Jogging is three times as fast so that would take him a third of the time: i.e. two hours. Thus he would save four hours by jogging home instead of walking.

53 From the answer he received, the Censor could tell that he wasn't dealing with a co-operative farmworker! However, he rolled his sleeves up and thought as follows: if he has N animals, $(N - 4)$ are bulls and $(N - 4)$ are cows, so he must have as many cows as he has bulls. He has at least one cow (he is milking it), so he must have at least one bull. It follows that he must have at least two horses. Of the four animals which are not cows, at most one is a bull. For, if there are as many horses as cattle, there must be twice as many horses as bulls. If there were two bulls, there would have to be four horses and thus *more* than four animals which were not cows. So the farmer has one bull only. He must therefore also have one cow. Since the number of horses equals the number of cattle, he must have two horses. As there are four animals which are not cows, there must also be a chicken. He has, therefore, one cow, one bull, two horses and a chicken.

55   She was a schoolteacher.

57   Miss Bathpale has as an anagram of her name: Miss
     Alphabet. This suggests looking at the letters of the fish
     names. She seems only to like those fish in whose names
     the vowels appear in the right order. Thus she ought, by
     this rule, to like halibut.   **A**

59   Note that in counting the last five steps he arrives at the
     landing. Therefore, when he has counted to 40, he has
     reached a point five stairs below the landing. Up to this
     point each five he has counted has corresponded to a net
     movement up the staircase of one stair. Thus before this
     point he has come up eight stairs. Thus there must be 13
     steps in all before the landing.

     I am unreliably informed that, on reaching the top, he
     would shout 'Happy Landing' and then parachute all the
     way down again.

61   A is 24 and B is 14. For 10 years ago, when B was four, A
     was 14. A is now six times as old as B was then. Two years
     before that, A was 12 and B was two, so A was then six
     times as old as B was then.

     Plantpott solved this puzzle along the lines suggested in
     the hint. He guessed that, on the earliest occasion referred
     to, B was two years old and so A was 12. Two years later B
     was four and A was 14. B must therefore be 14 now, and
     since this is 10 years later, A must now be 24. Now 24 (the
     age that A is now) is six times four (the age that B was
     when A was the age that B is now, i.e. 14) so this is indeed
     the answer.

     Having worked that out, Plantpott fell into a deep and
     satisfying sleep.   **A**

63   Starting with one amoeba in the jar, the number of
     amoebas in the jar will increase thus:

     Day: 1 2 3 4 5   6 etc.
     No: 1 2 4 8 16 32 etc.

     Starting with two amoebas would be equivalent to count-
     ing from Day 2 instead of from Day 1. Thus starting with
     two amoebas instead of one would save Dr Robe one whole
     day.

65 She cannot possibly do this.

If her average speed is to be doubled for the whole journey she must travel from Oxford to London and then from London to Oxford in exactly the same time that it took her to travel from Oxford to London! But whatever time it took her to travel from Oxford to London has been spent in doing just that. So unless she can drive from London to Oxford in no time at all she cannot realise her ambition.

To see this another way, suppose the distance from Oxford to London is exactly 60 miles. If she drives at an average speed of 30 miles per hour to London, the first leg of her journey takes two hours. If she wants her average speed for the *whole* journey to be 60 miles an hour, she must travel the 120 miles of the round trip in two hours. But these two hours have already been expended in driving to London. **A**

67 There are 100 houses in the street.

To solve this, note that along one side of the street the house numbers will increase by one as the corresponding house numbers on the other side decrease by one. The sum of the numbers of the two corresponding houses on opposite sides of the street must come to the same, which-ever pair of houses is chosen. House number 37 is opposite 64, therefore opposite house numbers must add up to 101. Therefore the number opposite number 1 must be 100 and this must be the last house in the street. Therefore there are 100 houses in the street. **A**

69 Yes. The needle will follow the groove in towards the spindle, because both sides of the disc have the same geometrical appearance when placed on the turntable. Thus replacing half of the A side by half of the B side will not alter the shape of the path the needle has to follow. It will, of course, play snatches of each side of shorter and shorter duration as the needle approaches the centre of the disc. **A**

71 Professor Tringle had set out not to confuse her children but had ended up confusing herself. If they are all wearing the wrong letters we must have either A wearing the letter B, B wearing the letter C and C wearing the letter A, or A wearing the letter C, B wearing the letter A and C wearing the letter B. But A addresses the brother wearing the letter B, so that he must be wearing the letter C. Therefore A is wearing the letter C, B is wearing the letter A and C is wearing the letter B.

73 *Facetiously* (in the question) or *abstemiously* (a clue is given in the way in which Striker behaved while trying to solve this).

75 The pipe cannot have cost £10 and the tobacco £1 or else the pipe would have cost only £9 more than the tobacco. The pipe must have cost £10.50 and the tobacco only 50p.

77 If there are $x + 1$ men in the team, x of them buy tickets (the goalkeeper being excluded from the calculations). They each buy x tickets so x^2 tickets are bought. If each costs p dinglies, then the money spent is x^2p, which, we know, equals 1,183 dinglies.

1,183 = 7×13^2, which suggests that $x = 13$ and $p = 7$. Thus, there are 13 men who buy tickets, which adding the forgetful goalkeeper, means there are 14 men in the team altogether. **A**

79 He smoked 19 and ⅓ cigarettes and had 58 smokes in all.

For there is only one stub left, which consists of ⅔ of a cigarette. If he had smoked every single third of a cigarette he would have had three times 20 smokes, i.e. 60 smokes. But he has left the final two smokes in the ashtray (the remaining stub) and so has had 58 smokes altogether.

In fact, his behaviour resulted in his smoking far more than he would have done if he'd just smoked them normally.

4 This is an old chestnut reheated.

6 Every number can be resolved into factors. If the only factors a number has are itself and 1, the number is said to be prime, e.g. 7 is a prime number, but 24 is not prime because: $24 = 6 \times 4$.

Any composite (non-prime) number can be resolved into factors which can be resolved in their turn until we end up with prime factors. Thus: $24 = 2 \times 2 \times 2 \times 3$ where all the numbers on the right are prime.

The set of prime numbers into which a number is resolved is unique. That is, 24 is the only number with 2, 2, 2 and 3 as its prime factors, and equally this is the only set of prime factors that 24 can be split into.

If a number is equal to the product of two prime numbers, it has no other factors. In this case, $118 = 2 \times 59$ and, as these are both prime numbers, they must be the *only* factors.

7 Consider the series: $1 + \frac{1}{2} + \frac{1}{4} + \frac{1}{8}$ etc. At each stage the difference between the sum and the number 2 decreases. That is, the more fractions we add to the sequence, the closer the sum approaches 2. Strictly speaking, it will never get there as there is always a difference left to halve. But this difference can be made as small as we wish, so that in the end it is negligible.

The perceptive reader will ask at this point how it is that jumblium can lay claim to being the 'bounciest of all substances' since it only bounced up to *half* the height of the previous bounce. The paradox is easily removed by pointing out that it exists in three forms. These are, in order of increasing bounciness, red, yellow and green. Puttylump's specimen was of red jumblium. The metals are used to colour the traffic lights on Zircon and since they are, in colour, closer to being orange, lemon and lime respectively, the natives of that planet speak of getting the lime-light instead of getting the green light. (See Hansoldt's *Whoopsy-Daisicon of Interplanetary Slang*.)

9   Pembish was not too slow to realise that, although he could fill the bath in this way, it was not a practical way of going about things. Since the hot tap is slower, the bath water would get colder and colder as the bath filled. To get the temperature of the bath constant one would need to have the hot and cold taps running at the same rate.

Also, since the combined rate of water flowing into the bath was greater than the rate at which it left via the plug-hole, the bath would overflow. In the end he adopted the following strategy: he turned both taps on full. After six minutes the bath was half-full. He then turned the cold tap until it was running at the same rate as the hot tap. Then water was entering the bath at the same rate as it was leaving via the plughole and so it stayed exactly half-full. Since the hot and cold taps were flowing at the same rate, the temperature settled down to a temperature intermediate between the hot and the cold water, i.e. tepid.

Luckily for him, the plug was discovered in the bread bin at this point and he was able to have a hot bath after all.

11 The ice-cube would fall without the buoyancy of the water, which must just balance the weight of the cube. Now, the amount of buoyancy must depend on the configuration of the water: i.e. the 'arrangement' of the water in the glass. (If you were to press the cube lower into the water the buoyancy would increase.)

We can see how much buoyancy the water supplies in Fig. 12. It would just support the weight of water displaced

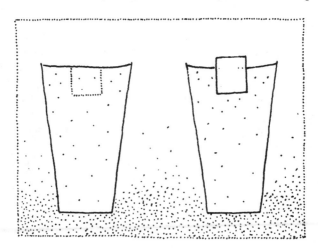

by the ice-cube up to the surface in the diagram, or, in other words, the ice-cube and the water which would fill up to the dotted line if the cube were removed have the same weight. This means if the ice-cube were to melt it would produce as much water as would fill up to the dotted line, and thus would not alter the level of the water.

Note that this argument applies only to the melting of ice which is afloat. If icebergs melt they do not affect the level of the sea. But if the polar ice-caps were to melt the water level would rise.

12 The boiling point of water is 212°F (100°C) and its freezing point is 32°F (0°C), so a change of 180° on the Fahrenheit scale is equivalent to a change of 100° on the Centigrade scale, that is, a change of 1°F is equivalent to a change of $\frac{5}{9}$°C.

The temperature in question must be below freezing point, for above freezing point the number of degrees Fahrenheit for a given temperature is always larger than the number of degrees Centigrade.

Suppose the answer is $-T$°C, then it must also be $-T$°F. Imagine cooling the jumblium from 32°F down to 0°F and then down to $-T$°F. This represents a cooling through $(32 + T)$ Fahrenheit degrees. Each of these Fahrenheit degrees corresponds to $\frac{5}{9}$ Centigrade degrees.

So the temperature is: $\frac{5}{9} \times (32 + T)$°C below zero, or: $\frac{5}{9} (32 + T) = T$. Multiplying both sides by 9 gives: $5 (32 + T) = 9T$, or: $160 + 5T = 9T$, whence $T = 40$. Therefore the temperature in question is 40°C below zero, i.e. -40°C or -40°F.

15 More cumbersomely: if N be the number of eggs each hen
lays in a day and H the number of hens the farmer has,
then Puttylump has to solve the equation:

$$H^N = N^H$$

He knows that N and H must be integers as neither
chickens nor eggs (no matter which came first) come in
fractions. He discards the possibility that $N = 1$, otherwise
there would be only one rather unremarkable hen, and
anyway the farmer speaks of his charges as 'these 'ens'.

He also discards the possibility that $N = H$. Then the
equation would read:

$$H^H = H^H$$

which is true for all values of H, but there would be no
change in the economy of feeding the hens if the number of
hens and the number of eggs they each laid per day were
interchanged.

Taking the next possible value for N, try $N = 2$. The
equation becomes:

$$H^2 = 2^H$$

As the number on the right of this equation is even (since it
is a power of 2), the number on the left-hand side must be
even too. It follows that H must be even. Since H cannot be
2, we try the next even number, which is 4:

$$4^2 = 2^4$$

which is indeed true.

Thus, he has either two hens laying four eggs each per day,
or four hens laying two eggs each per day. Either way they
together lay eight eggs a day, but clearly, as it would be
cheaper from the point of view of feeding them if there
were two hens laying four eggs, the farmer must in fact
have four hens laying two eggs each per day.

It is possible to prove mathematically that this is the *only*
solution, but the proof is too long-winded for our present
purposes.

17 This is another old chestnut. 'Zolot', by the way, means 'gold'.

20 Let the required number be x. Then:

$$\frac{x + 1}{x + 4} = \tfrac{2}{3}$$

Cross-multiplying:

$$3\,(x + 1) = 2\,(x + 4)$$
$$3x + 3 = 2x + 8$$
$$x = 5$$

Note that the fractional equation at the beginning of this solution cannot be solved by merely setting $x + 1 = 2$ and $x + 4 = 3$.

21 Polish pronunciation is not as bad as all that. Some other English words have six consecutive consonants, e.g. watchstrap, Hampsthwaite. In Serbo-Croat (or in Srpskohrvatski, as it is called in Yugoslavia), some words have no written vowels at all, e.g. krk (a place), crn (black), vrt (garden), trvd (hard) or prst (finger).

23 Stars' brother is called TIMOTHY. His friends have nicknamed him MOTHS as he collects insects. So far, he has 17 of them.

24 Her name was HEIDI.

26 If the digits of her age are A and B, her age is written AB which stands for $10A + B$ years. Her age reversed is BA and this stands for $10B + A$ years. Adding these together gives:

$$11A + 11B = 11\,(A + B)$$

Thus the result of a calculation of this sort is always divisible by 11. The other number therefore by which the result is divisible must be equal to $(A + B)$. Stars knows that $(A + B)$ is 10. The only number less than 28 whose digits can be reversed and added to the original number to satisfy this is 19. This was the age of the undergraduette.

27 See Appendix 26.

29 In fact, he was so embarrassed he almost had a 'nihil ex nihilp fit'.

30 If we can only add together numbers of the form A and AB where A and B are digits, the task is impossible. To see this, note that the sum of all the digits is 45 and this is obviously too little to amount to 100 as its stands. We need to take some of these digits and use them to stand for tens. Suppose we use the digits $X, Y, Z, \ldots$ for the tens' place, then the sum of the digits will be $45 - (X + Y + Z + \ldots)$. The tens' column will represent $10 (X + Y + Z \ldots)$. Putting the two together:

$$10 (X + Y + Z + \ldots) + 45 - (X + Y + Z + \ldots)$$
$$= 45 + 9(X + Y + Z + \ldots)$$

This is the number we hope to make equal to 100. Setting it equal to 100, we get:

$$100 = 45 + 9 (X + Y + Z + \ldots)$$

i.e. $\frac{55}{9} = (X + Y + Z \ldots)$

But $\frac{55}{9}$ is not a whole number and the right-hand side *is* a whole number (since it consists of a sum of digits). A whole number cannot be equal to a non-whole number. Therefore, it is not possible to add together numbers of the form 7, 2, 45, 68 etc. using all the digits from 0 to 9 once only and arrive at 100.

31 To see this, imagine a table of all the numbers which can be formed by using two of the digits: 0, 1, 2, 3, 4, 5, 6, 7, 8, 9.

These will start from 00 and end at 99. There are 100 such numbers and each digit appears 20 times in all.

However, as we do not write 01, 02 . . . 09, we can subtract nine zeroes from the tally. Secondly, we do not wish to include the two zeroes in 00. But the table also doesn't include 100, which requires an extra one and two zeroes. Thus, all in all, for the numbers from 1 to 100, we need 11 zeroes and 21 ones. The other digits occur 20 times each.

35 People who colour their socks in this way are a dying breed.

43 If A has age a now and B has age $(a + x)$, then in x years time A will be the age that B is now. Also, x years ago, B was the age A is now. Making a table of ages will look as follows:

	Past	Present	Future
A:	$a - x$	a	$a + x$
B:	a	$a + x$	$a + 2x$

We see that A's statement amounts to saying that: $(a + 2x) = 3 (a - x)$. Multiplying this out gives: $a + 2x = 3a - 3x$. This then gives $x = \frac{2}{5}a$. But both a and x are whole numbers. Since x is an integer, a must be divisible by 5. The smaller we choose a, the younger the interlocutors. The smallest number divisible by 5 is 5. So a is 5 and x is 2.

From this we see that A is five years old and B is seven.

46 The argument about 'either side' continued well into the afternoon. Punnish pointed out that a Christmas cracker can be pulled from either end although, of course, it has to be pulled from both. Then Pembish suggested, rather impishly, that Punnish try and stand on either end of a fruit ladder. In the end they both agreed to put the matter (and the cannonballs) to one side.

47 An integer (whole number) into which each of a set of integers will divide an integral number of times is called a common multiple. Thus 140 is a common multiple of 2, 5 and 7. So is 420. The lowest common multiple is the smallest multiple that the set of numbers have in common, e.g. the lowest common multiple of 2, 5 and 7 is 70. To deduce the lowest common multiple of a set of numbers, first reduce them to prime factors. Then work out the product of all the prime factors of these numbers, repeated as many times as they each appear in the number in which they appear the most. To find the lowest common multiple for the three numbers 24, 126 and 105 break them down into prime factors:

$24 = 2 \times 2 \times 2 \times 3$
$126 = 2 \times 3 \times 3 \times 7$
$105 = 3 \times 5 \times 7$

Thus, the lowest common multiple is
$2 \times 2 \times 2 \times 3 \times 3 \times 5 \times 7$. This equals 2,520.

49 Punnish's frustration was no doubt due to the fact that the clock did not know its place in the scheme of things: he was meant to be winding it up, and not vice versa.

57 Although it was perfectly rational for Miss Grammatica to assume that there was some rule to Miss Bathpale's likes and dislikes, nothing in life ever runs so smoothly. It turned out that Miss Bathpale detests halibut, so, if there was a rule, this was an exception.

61 We know that A is older than B. Suppose that on the first of the three occasions mentioned (in chronological order), the age of A was a and B's age was $(a - x)$. Two years later their ages were $(a + 2)$ and $(a - x + 2)$ respectively. If this second period refers to the time when A was the same age as B is now, B's age now must be $(a + 2)$. The third and last occasion (the present) is x years later than the second.

It is easiest to write this in tabular form:

	Now	Before	Two years before that
A:	$(a + 2 + x)$	$(a + 2)$	a
B:	$(a + 2)$	$(a - x + 2)$	$(a - x)$

From A's first remark: $(a + 2 + x) = 6 (a - x + 2)$. The right-hand bracket of this equation extends to: $6a - 6x + 12$, which simplifies to: $5a + 10 = 7x$.

From B's remark: $a = 6 (a - x)$. This leads to: $5a = 6x$. Substituting this value for $5a$ into the first equation we get $5a + 10 = 7x$, gives $6x + 10 = 7x$, which simplifies to $x = 10$. Now $5a = 6x = 60$, so $a = 12$. A's age now is $(a + 2 + x)$ which equals 24, and B's age is $(a + 2)$ which equals 14.

64 This does not prove that there wouldn't be enough room for 13 or more ping-pong balls to fit in a cluster around the inner one. But certainly no-one has yet managed to cluster more than 12 balls around and in direct contact with a central ball of the same size.

65 To show this algebraically, let the distance between London and Oxford be x miles and the time taken to travel from Oxford to London be t hours, then: $30 = x/t$. For the total journey, there and back, let the time be: $(t + T)$. Now we require: $60 = 2x/(t + T)$. That is, $30 = x/(t + T)$. But $30 = x/t$ already. So this means $T = 0$, or, in other words, that the return journey must take no time.

67 Minkweet St (on the label of the parcel in the illustration) is an anagram of Kitten Mews.

68 Suppose the time was *H* hours and *y* minutes. Each whole hour corresponds to a movement of the little hand of five minute-divisions, i.e. at exactly *H* o'clock, the little hand points to 5*H* minutes. If the minute hand is not on the 12 of the clock-face, we must add a minute-division to the result of the position of the hour hand for each 12 minutes it is past the hour. Therefore, if the time is *H* hours and *y* minutes, the minute hand points to *y* and the hour hand points to 5*H* plus $y/12$.

In the question, the hour hand is exactly 13 minutes behind the minute hand, so:

$$5H + y/12 + 13 = y$$

This can be tidied up to give:

$$5H + 13 = 11y/12$$
i.e. $5H = 11y/12 - 13$

Now *H* must be a whole number (or integer), so *y* must be one too. Therefore *y* must be divisible by 12. Also *y* must be less than 60 (as this is the total number of minutes on the clock-face), so we need only try out multiples of 12 less than 60. This leaves the possibilities:

$$y = 12, 24, 36, 48$$
$$\text{If } y = 12, 5H = -2$$
$$\text{If } y = 24, 5H = 9$$
$$\text{If } y = 36, 5H = 20$$
$$\text{If } y = 48, 5H = 31$$

The only one of these combinations which would give *H* as an integral number is the third one. Therefore: *H* = 4 and *y* = 36. Thus the time was 4.36 precisely.

69 A pity it wasn't Stockhausen.

72 Some people think the answer to this puzzle should consist in pointing out that cockerels do not lay eggs. That is just begging the question.

74 Imagine a bolt in a nut. Cut through one of the sides of the nut and imagine little by little straightening it and turning it inside out, in such a way that its thread still touches the bolt. Then one would eventually arrive at the state of affairs when the thread of the nut was on the outside and was still in contact with the bolt. The handedness of the thread is not changed during this process, and the bolt would move in the same direction if wound along the nut as if the nut was in its original form. In its original form, turning the bolt clockwise from one side has the same effect as turning the nut anticlockwise from the other. It follows that two bolts, when twiddled by Didipotamus in this way, move towards each other, for they are identical in this respect to a matching bolt and nut.

77 If 1,183 is resolved into prime factors (see also Appendix 6) we obtain: $1,183 = 7 \times 13 \times 13$. Since these are all prime factors, this is the only possible way to break down 1,183. We require: $x^2p = 7 \times 13 \times 13$. As p and x have to be integers, x has to be 13 and p has to be 7.